MOM, CAN I DO MY LAUNDRY AT YOUR HOUSE?

MOM, CAN I DO MY LAUNDRY AT YOUR HOUSE?

POEMS FROM YOUR ADULT CHILD

By Olivia Roberts

CHRONICLE BOOKS

SAN FRANCISCO

Library of Congress Cataloging-in-Publication Data

Names: Roberts, Olivia, 1994- author.

Title: Mom, can I do my laundry at your house? : poems from
your adult child / by Olivia Roberts.

Description: San Francisco : Chronicle Books, [2023]

Identifiers: LCCN 2022034306 | ISBN 9781797218694 (hardback)

Subjects: LCSH: Mothers--Poetry. | LCGFT: Humorous poetry.

Classification: LCC PS3618.O3158746 M66 2023 | DDC

811/.6--dc23/eng/20220805

LC record available at https://lccn.loc.gov/2022034306

Manufactured in China.

Illustrations and design by Maggie Edelman.

10 9 8 7 6 5 4 3 2 1

Chronicle Books LLC
680 Second Street
San Francisco, CA 94107
www.chroniclebooks.com

This book is dedicated to moms everywhere,
but especially *you*!

To: _____

From: _____

Thank you for being my mom.

Thank you for everything you have given me

A roof over my head

A bed to sleep in

An education and all the skills I need to be an independent adult

Anyway, can I do my laundry at your house?

Oh excellent,

You've gone grocery shopping

Which means I, too, can go grocery shopping

In your pantry

Thank you for visiting my apartment

And not saying a word about the mess

Even though you really wanted to

That must have taken a lot of strength

I want to call you all the time

When something good has happened at work

When I use that cooking trick you taught me

When I see a mom and their child at the store

When I use your Netflix account

And yet I only call you when I am in crisis

I haven't eaten a vegetable in years

But I am aware of the fact that they are integral to a healthy diet

And that part is all thanks to you

Sorry about that time I listened to "Complicated" by Avril Lavigne on repeat for a week when I was 10

My life was not that complicated and I see that now

You are amazing, kind, patient, and beautiful

This one isn't a funny poem

It's just true

A mother was raising a daughter

But the girl resisted and fought her

There once came a day

When the girl said, Oh hey

Now she appreciates all her mom taught her

Remember that time I begged you to buy me that shirt?

And you said, Only if you promise to wear it?

I never wore it

Thanks for giving me the recipe for our family's secret marinara sauce

Next time you make it, can you please drop some off at my house?

I see that you're typing

And I will wait patiently for your text to come through

Because I know

You are only using

Your pointer finger

I can always count on you to have

AN ENTIRE PHARMACY

In your purse

Just in case

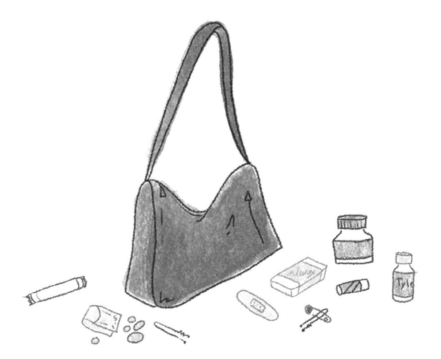

Why is your skin always so soft

Is that a mom thing?

Sorry I expected you to be a professional hairdresser

That shit is hard

You're not *always* right

But you are right 98% of the time

Here is a haiku

It's a poetry book, right?

I love you a lot

Oh wow

Looks like I called you for some advice

Again

For the fifth time today

I'm sure you spent your hard-earned money to
buy a house

And you meticulously decorated it

And kept it clean and organized

Just for some stupid eleven-year-old to wallpaper
their bedroom with photos of Pete Wentz

Why do you have thirty wooden spoons in your kitchen drawer?

When I was little

We had something called the Trust Bank

Any time I would do something bad

I would lose your trust

And you would call it "making a withdrawal"

Honestly

Pretty good metaphor

I might start telling my idiot boyfriend about his
withdrawals from the Trust Bank

It was very cool of you to let me play my music in the car

Even when I was going through my screamo phase

Everyone has tattoos now, Mom

Maybe we should get one together

☐ Yes   ☐ No   ☐ Don't tell Dad

Thank you for helping me with my homework

Except math

Being bad at math must be genetic

When I was young I thought you were an invincible
superhero

Now I realize you are just a h u m a n

  and you have human feelings

  and make human mistakes

  and do all the other human things just like everyone else

You're still a superhero to me anyway

When I hate someone

You hate someone

That's loyal as hell

It's nice that we agree on the Beatles

You taught me to handle conflict

Calmly

Rationally

Efficiently

And without violence

That's great and all but

I am going to fight every single person

Who has ever been mean to you

Some days

All I want to do

Is hang out with you

Once again

I lay awake last night

Thinking about all the stupid things I did to you as a
teenager

And felt

G U I L T

Until I remembered you wouldn't let me go to Parker
Logan-Lewis's 8th grade graduation party

I know you have insecurities just like everybody else

But you are one of the most wonderful, beautiful,
sweetest people I have ever met

And I hate that you don't think so

M agnanimous

O pen-minded

T houghtful

H onest

E mpathetic

R eally good at folding a fitted sheet no seriously how
do you do it

That time I was 2 years old

And tried to attack my brother with a baseball bat

Must have been very stressful for you

Luckily

I was 2 years old

And couldn't really hold a baseball bat

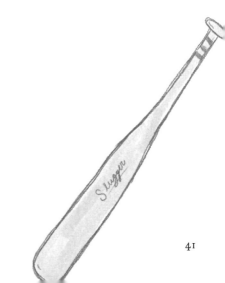

Thank you for being funny

Because it means I am funny

Can you even imagine *not* being funny?

Gross

Oh!

How I cannot believe

You have had such strength

To put up with me and my bullshit

I'm glad

We can go on vacation now

As equals

But you've got the dinner bill, right?

How did you not yell at me way more?

I mean

T h a n k   y o u   for not yelling at me

But

    d

        a

            m

                n

I was annoying

I promise not to tell Dad about your crush on The Rock

EVERY

SINGLE

DAY

I remember how lucky I am

That I am able to call you my mom

I grew up and I realized

You don't know everything

But let's be real

Don't you, though?

Did you also find it super awkward

When we watched *Chocolat* together

When I was 12

I am starting

To understand

Why

On family trips

You needed to stop for a bathroom break every two
seconds

Because now I

Have to stop for a bathroom break every two seconds

Hark! You have finally figured out memes!

If I could be at least half as patient as you

Maybe I would actually fold my laundry after washing it

In fact

I think I'm SUPPOSED to be half as patient as you

As I am technically half of you

Regardless

The laundry stays unfolded

Oh yeah,

Can you tell Dad

I love him, too

I'm sure it must have been very annoying

When I went through my

Scared-of-escalators phase

Long-distance runners deserve their Olympic medals,
I guess

But it's hard to find them all that impressive

When you have played the ultimate long game

You love me now

But you also loved me when I was being a huge brat
from about 2002 until 2012

Talk about stamina

I'm scared of spiders

You're scared of spiders

We're all scared of spiders

And yet the way you would kill them for me anyway
Is the most selfless and heroic thing I've ever seen

You gave me everything

I gave you this book

Okay, okay

I'll do laundry at home this week

Because I am an adult

But do you have any quarters?

Seriously though

In case
You could
Not tell

I love you, Mom